AF434903

THE WAR
YOU THINK

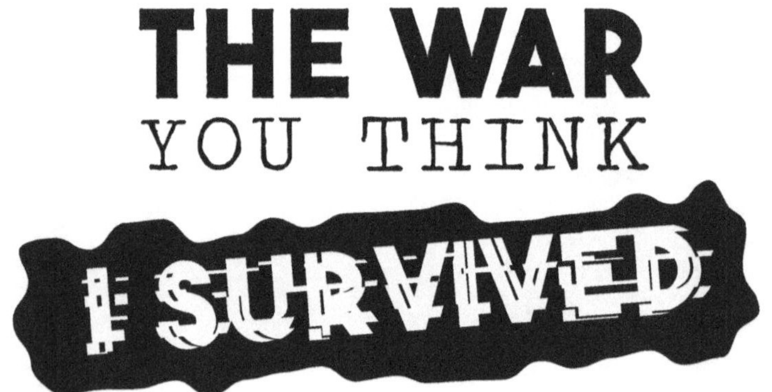

Asmaa Althami

The War You Think I Survived

© 2024 Asmaa Althami

Cover Design & Illustartion © Asmadsgns.com

Edited: By Jon Roemer

Dear Shatha,

I have a confession to make about why
I didn't take your advice not to write
about war, and it's not that I found
your advice lacking. But there's a
story waiting to be painted, the one
you started but never got to finish.

—Asmaa

Acknowledgments

First and foremost, I want to express my deepest appreciation to my beloved husband for his unwavering support and encouragement throughout the journey of writing this book.

I also extend my heartfelt gratitude to Jon Roemoer for his exceptional editing skills and insightful suggestions that significantly enriched this manuscript.

Special thanks to Dr. Laura Huisinga, my cherished professor, whose guidance, provision of valuable resources, and feedback were
invaluable throughout the entire writing process.

I am profoundly grateful for the contributions of these remarkable individuals, whose support has made this book possible.

Contents

Why I'm Writing This book 10

Disclaimer: This book is not political 13

How did it all begin? 16

Losing track of time............................ 19

April 20, 2015 24

The unknown destination 27

Our Reality vs. Media Narratives 30

Alternative lifestyle 33

Crossing the border 36

Returning to Sanaa 42

Drowning 43

Cairo 48

Now what?............................ 53

Fun City 57

I suddenly remembered "Shams"............................61

What is home? 64

Weeks turned into months and months into years.......67

My Wedding Day............................70

Coming back to US............................72

Have I ever survived war?............................76

WAR WAR
WAR WAR WAR
WAR WAR WAR
WAR WAR WAR
WAR WAR WAR
WAR WAR WAR WAR
WAR WAR WAR WAR
WAR WAR WAR

I'll Keep writting about war untill it loses it's power

Why I'm Writing This book

I recently had a conversation with my friend Shatha, someone with whom I share not just a profound conection but a parallel tapestry of life experiences. She warned me against the journey I was about to embark upon writing about war. She recounted trying to paint a war-inspired project for a college assignment. As she immersed herself in the haunting images, a wave of trauma engulfed her, leaving the canvas incomplete. Her ability to express herself artistically was stifled forever.

It's this fear that drives me to write about war—the fear that war itself might inhibit me from expressing its impact on me. The fear of always being defeated by war. The fear of war always being larger, stronger, and unstoppable. The fear of being overwhelmed by emotions, just like Shatha, and being unable to complete this book, drives me to write even more. This book is my way of seeking revenge on war by exposing its ugliness, making it appear smaller, uglier, and weaker.

For a time, I even avoided saying the word "war" because I
didn't want to confront the emotions it stirred within me.
It frustrated me that a single word could hold so much power
over me, leaving me speechless and unable to express myself.

But in a time when graphic war images dominate the media, I've
chosen not to showcase violence, but rather to portray
everyday life before, during, and after war.
These all-to-common experiences must be acknowledged, along
with the violence sensationalized by the media. I refuse to let
the detached and fragmented analysis of cable news networks
tell the only stories we hear. And I refuse to be afraid of what
this confrontation could do to me, to fear the creative spirit I risk
stifling here.

So here I am, nearly a decade later, beginning this
journey not just as an observer, but as a witness and
a storyteller, striving
to echo silenced voices. It's a pursuit borne not out of
naivete, but out of the belief that stories have the power to
illuminate, humanize, and foster understanding in the face of the
shadows cast by war.

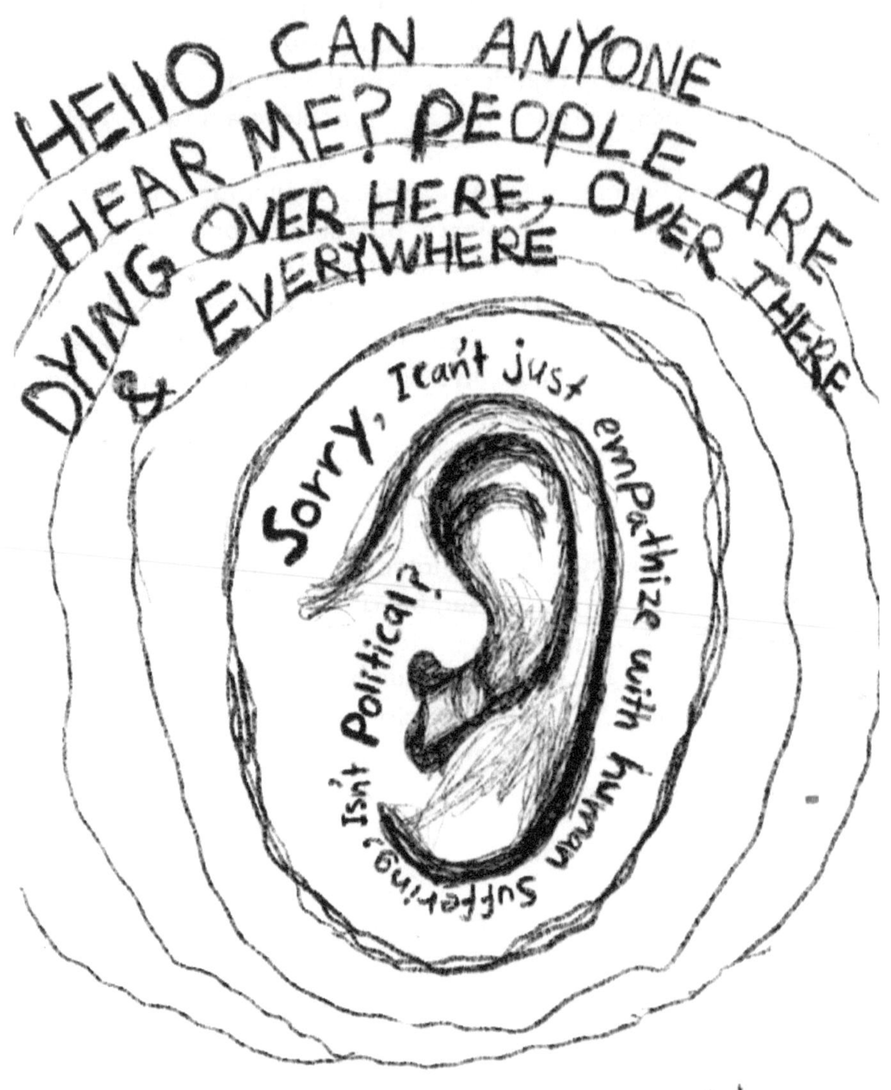
HELLO CAN ANYONE HEAR ME? PEOPLE ARE DYING OVER HERE, OVER THERE & EVERYWHERE
Sorry, I can't just empathize with human suffering? Isn't political?
This might seem "political" & I don't do politics

Disclaimer: This book is not political

Undertaking the task of writing this book and revisiting my war diaries, I've made a rather groundbreaking decision.
Brace yourselves – this won't be a political book.

Shocking, right? Despite being a very "political" person, or maybe because my life has been so deeply impacted by others' politics, I usually don't have the luxury of avoiding it. Beyond that, I'm perpetually seen as political; blame it on my appearance or the way I casually discuss the tragic losses of my people – everything about me gets stamped with a political label, whether I ask for it or not.But within the pages of this book, I'm attempting the monumental task of keeping politics at bay. (Well, I'll give it my best shot.)

I understand why some people avoid talking about politics. It's challenging, even exhausting when seemingly mundane things like wearing or not wearing a mask during COVID-19 are viewed through a political lens. Questions arise about who defines these rules, what is considered political, and why are conversations about human rights and social justice increasingly perceived as political?

Labeling basic human rights as "political" often results in not discussing them at all, including the harsh realities of war.
I get it—some folks genuinely want to listen, but the mere whiff of anything political triggers an imaginary
earplug response.

This book is about creating a bold space where criosity can triumph over suspicions or reservations, allowing a deep dive into the raw, human side of war. The primary spotlight is on the unfiltered human experience of residing in a war zone, to create a true understanding of and connection with the human aspect of war. Politics has its place, providing logic and frameworks (sometimes), but it rarely aligns with the lived reality of those enduring the wars.The aim is to invite readers, espcially those hesitant about political discussions, to approach this book fearlessly, to ensure that the unfiltered experiences of war reach people without unnecessary apprehension.

Now, picture this: constant bombardment, no electricity, and water shortages, life-transforming into a perplexing puzzle. Contrast this with someone on the other side of the world, impeccably dressed, seated in a well-lit cable network studio, discussing and explaining why this war should make sense. The disparity feels surreal, almost dystopian, especially when your life is hanging
by a thread.

In writing this book, I intend to dismantle these barriers, to lay bare the genuine, human moments of surviving the unimaginable. This is also not just a recounting of events; it's an earnest attempt to bridge the gap between the abstract discussions of war and the raw, lived experiences of those enduring its brutal realities. The stories within these pages seek to humanize, to bring forth the emotions, struggles and resilience of individuals navigating the unfathomable challenges of war.

How did it all begin?

On the night of March 27, 2015, I distinctly recall not feeling well and going to bed at the unusually late hour of 2 am. The airstrikes that soon unfolded in those early hours went unnoticed—at least by me, lost in the depths of my slumber. I woke up in the morning feeling better, ready for another college day. But the house felt a bit off. My Grandma was visiting the day before and decided to stay that night. She usually liked to sleep upstairs whenever she came over but seemed to sleep downstairs with her door open that night. Odd vibes, but no one was up to explain.

When I was about to leave, I also saw my parents' door open. My dad, half-asleep, heard the sound of my car keys and called after me: "Asmaa, don't go today!" I went back to my room and really wanted to ask him why, but he was so sleepy and I didn't want to bother. Lots of questions, but everyone was still asleep.

I decided to kill some time by browsing Facebook, and there it was—flags of ten countries, announcing air strikes and starting a war in Sana'a, Yemen. Air strikes? Sounded unreal, but after confirming, it was shockingly true. What does war even mean? I'm set to graduate with my bachelor's in two semesters!

I always thought war was something you see on the news, in movies, or only hear about, not something you live through. Maybe I was so detached from reality because, even though I was living in Yemen at the time – a country often labeled as the poorest in the Middle East—it wasn't my reality. My family and I lived comfortably in a 10-bedroom house, which might sound like a mansion from an American perspective. At 18, I had my own car, which my dad had paid for. I attended an international university, which is relatively more expensive than other options in Yemen.

I was just living life, like you, like most Americans, never imagining that war was supposed to happen to me. So many questions flooded my mind the minute I saw that Facebook post. Is this really happening? Are we going to be safe? Will my university close? Am I even still a student, and what does this mean for everyone else in my house?

why bother tracking time when it's still
& sun hides away, silent & chill
wether we're in bed for hours or days
Does it really matter in an endless maze

Losing track of time

The first thing that I remember in the first days of war is just losing track of time. Time slipped away. The absence of electricity plunged us into prolonged darkness, amplifying the sense of eternal darkness.

My college closed its doors, everything came to a standstill, and going outside was no longer safe. It kinda looked like the coronavirus quarantine era, but with the additional challenges of no electricity, water scarcity, no internet access, and consistent bombing. We used to keep an electrical generator in our backyard because brief power outages were somewhat common in Yemen. Once the war began, these interruptions became more frequent, occurring for over 10 hours a day. But even our reliable generator became useless when fuel became scarce due to the blockade. A small water bottle-sized container of gas skyrocketed to $100 USD on the black market, and even if it we could afford it, acquiring one became an arduous task.

Over time, we adopted alternative solutions, like extracting gas from our cars! When we ran out of fuel from cars, our backup plan was car batteries—not to light up the entire house, but just enough to power the Wi-Fi and stay
connected to the outside world.

Even something as basic as going to the bathroom became a challenge; with no water flowing through the pipes, we had to rely on emergency reserves. Without going into too much detail, managing a bathroom without water was quite inconvenient. Due to the limited supply, flushing sometimes became a luxury.

During those days of plugging into car batteries, we would check the news to get insights into when the situation might improve. Initially, they spoke of a two-week operation named "Decisive Storm." But two weeks stretched into months,and months transformed into eight years of enduring war!

"Dear Diary,
it's been about a month or so I think. Time has slipped away, and the days meld into a blur. The atmosphere carries a heavy silence, and darkness wraps around everything. The explosions echo loudly, casting Sana'a into a realm without light or water. The life we once knew has faded into the shadows.

Two days ago, while standing in the middle of the kitchen, an unexpected and formidable suction of air enveloped the space. The sensation, though unnerving, has become a familiar dance with danger.

I've learned to figure out if it's close or far based on that air pull caused by changes in pressure. Immediately after that feeling, the explosion happened, shaking everything in its wake.

A powerful gust of wind ensued, so forceful it shoved me across our kitchen. At that moment, I heard things breaking in different rooms and glass shattering. I held onto my mom tightly, and somehow, we managed to get through it.

When the sun rose after such a crazy night, I felt incredibly alive, especially after being so close to death. That morning, I could almost feel every vein pulsating in my body.

I decided to go out and reconnect with my creative self, because I heard some places were opening up. I was excited to get some acrylic paint. Even with all the changes going on, there are still things that bring me joy and that I refuse to give up.

Strolling through the streets that were once bustling with life, I was met with an unsettling emptiness. The once vibrant atmosphere had vanished, transforming Sana'a into a ghost town.

As I moved along, I noticed shiny bits on the ground,but it wasn't glitter like I thought — it was broken glass from houses and buildings. Witnessing the extent of destruction that unfolded in just a month weighed heavily on my heart, and I found myself yearning to stay home for another month or even a year.The reality outside was far from what I had anticipated."

84 civilians were
Killed with their hopes
& dreams
600 were
injured
Sanáa, Yemen
April 20, 2015

April 20, 2015

This date is etched in the memory of everyone who lived in Sana'a – a day of horror that each person has their own story about. My story began when I woke up for breakfast:

"As I woke up to prepare breakfast, the morning took a horrifying turn. A powerful missile shattered our peaceful meal, making my eyeglasses fly off my face and plunging us into chaos. Unable to comprehend the situation or the origin of the explosion, we found ourselves on the ground, my mom, my youngest twin sisters and me. Behind us a massive TV and entertainment center, with glass cabinet doors and heavy decorations, trembled and tilted perilously, almost crashing down on us. Closing my eyes, I braced for the worst, but thank god it stayed in its place.

Facing the stairs is our large window, a Yemeni architectural feature known as "Manwar" (derived from the Arabic word "Noor," meaning light), typically designed to allow light into the staris. With the blast that morning, part of this huge window shattered into small, knife—like pieces, and as my dad was ascending the stairs to join us, he sustained an injury from a shard into his thigh.

Fortunately, it only struck his upper leg, and a few inches either way could have led to a more disastrous outcome. My brother was sleeping downstairs, and he woke up to tiny clouds of debris falling from the ceiling. Since he was still half—asleep, he initially thought it was smoke and couldn't comprehend what was happening.

The explosion was so loud that I couldn't feel my ears because of the pressure. My twin sisters were screaming at the top of their lungs, and that hurt me deeply. At just six years old, they witnessed more horrible things than I have in my 20 years. They'd felt what it's like to almost die several times by then, which is heartbreaking. After that happened, we packed quickly and left the house, but where were we going?"

Drive me
to the unknown,
for the familiar
no longer feels
like home

The unknown destination

I clearly remember us being completely clueless about where we were headed. My dad, multitasking, was making a ton of phone calls while navigating the road. He was on a mission to find a safer place for our family. I distinctly remember him having a lengthyconversation with my uncle because they were in a similar situation near a targeted mountain, just like us.

After some back-and-forth, they managed to find a place about 5 miles away. The selling point? You could hear the airstrikes but not feel them. It became our newfound destination, and as we began on our journey— my dad, my youngest brother, my mom and my twin sisters joining my uncle, grandma, three aunts and two cousins who had already settled in the same apartment we were heading to.

"Dear Diary,
Today was like something out of a nightmare. As we left our house, the mountain loomed in the distance, still burning like an erupting volcano. Mariam, my sister, whispered in a melancholy tone, "Everything is destroyed."

The aftermath of the explosion unveiled itself on our way. Even distant areas bore the scars, shattered glass attesting to the force of the blast. We found refuge in an unfurnished place, chosen not for its amenities but for the security it promised compared to our own house. Three bedrooms and one bathroom for the thirteen of us — it's tight, but at least it's safe.

The clock now reads nine, and here we are in the darkness, devoid of electricity. It's eerie, isolating. The absence of TV, lights, and even the internet heightens the unease. I reached out to some close friends, desperately needing a connection in this disconnection, finding solace in the news that they're okay."

I Was On Screen
but my screams were quiet...
Emotionless, silent, or out of sight
I Was there,
yet my pain remained unseen
a silent presence on a digital screen ...

Our Reality vs. Media Narratives

I recall watching the explosion videos near our old house a few days later. They were truly disturbing. Many people in Sanaa shared these videos, and they quickly went viral. They were horrific because it felt like it could have been me in those videos.

Each video showed the same explosion from various angles. Some were close to the explosion and glitched before stopping abruptly, leaving a chilling silence. The sounds of people panicking and running away, followed by the sudden silence in some videos, hinted that the person recording might not have made it. It was bothersome and left a lasting impact.

In one of the videos, a father was recording what happened. He knew from the sight of the massive explosion that the sound and shockwave would follow, so he tried to calm his children with a shaky voice, saying, "Please don't panic, please don't panic." As soon as the sound erupted and windows shattered, he screamed at the top of his lungs for his kids to run away.

I also remember watching the same scene on television, broadcasted by a non-Yemeni station that typically depicted the war as strategic and only affecting "targets." They used the same video and took advantage of the fact that no one appeared in it, making it seem like it wasn't filmed inside a civilian house. They muted the sound of the father's desperate cries, concealing the reality that this war was impacting civilians more than anyone else.

Not only did we have to endure the hardships of the war itself, but we also faced the additional challenge of our stories and suffering being misrepresented right before our eyes, with people believing those who held more power. It was deeply saddening to witness, leading me to question how many other truths were being hidden in the same way.

Alternative lifestyle

Let me take you deeper into the saga of our cramped yet somehow cozy existence in that 3-bedroom, 1-bathroom apartment housing all thirteen of us. You can almost feel the squeeze. It was in a 2-story house where the owner lived on the second floor and left the first floor empty, which we decided to rent.

That place was devoid of the essentials — no beds, couches, or a carpet. Our improvised seating and sleeping arrangements relied on hastily brought blankets from home. The bathroom situation was a constant frenzy, with a never-ending knock on the door as someone eagerly waited their turn. The dream of taking a 10-minute bath quickly faded. Bathing itself turned into a laborious task, given the dependence on an electricity-reliant water heater. We had to resort to traditional methods, like heating water on the stove and carefully carrying the pot to the bathroom, adding an extra layer of complexity to our daily routines.

Navigating the limited personal space was a significant challenge for someone accustomed to having her own room and bathroom. But even in the squeeze, we found positive aspects. Those three months became a period of deep bonding. Our meals, though basic, were cooked in one or two pots due to our limited kitchen tools. Gathered around a single large plate, we engaged in conversations spanning generations, creating enduring memories. Together, we relied on simple pleasures, like our daily afternoon ritual of sipping Adani chai and sending a child to the nearby store for biscuits or cake to pair with it. And then there were the backyard adventures. The younger ones, my sisters and cousins, brought an undeniable atmosphere of joy. And yet it was tinged with bittersweetness, watching them play games that mimicked the sounds of airstrikes. They'd debate whether it was a Scud missile, like the one that struck Faj Attan mountain, prompting our evacuation. Mixed emotions colored our days,intensified by the unsettling news of friends and family fleeing the country. It was a time defined by the unspoken strength found in shared hardship.

As the war dragged on, people realized the need to adapt. I remember an internet store offering Wi-Fi access for limited time slots (about 2 hours a day). I have no idea how they made that work, but it was a lifesaver for staying connected, downloading books, and playing 8-ball pool online with friends as a way to pass the time. Yemenis have always been incredibly adaptable and capable of creating solutions out of necessity. It's difficult to determine whether this adaptability is ultimately positive or negative.

You might wonder why I see adaptability as a downside. Well, when we constantly adjust to tough situations without seeking improvement or change, we end up unintentionally prolonging them. Also, too much adaptability can make people forget their worth in the long run. It's like we settle for less than we deserve and lose sight of our true value and potential.

Not a Fun fact

I walked in desert once
until my feet bled

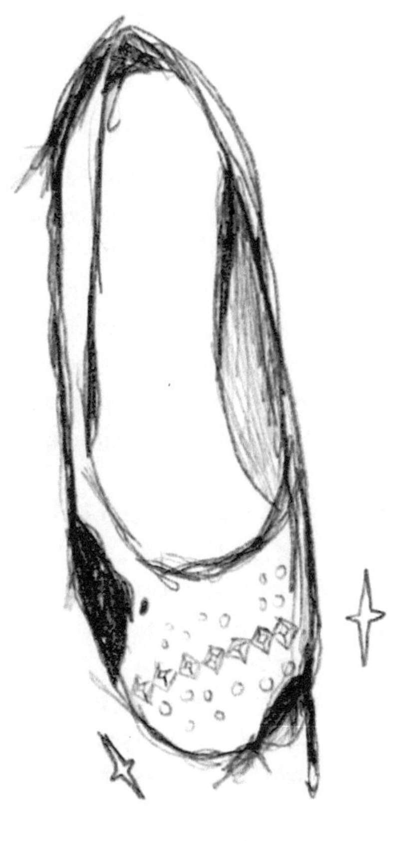

Crossing the border

Three months into the war, my family of twelve and I found ourselves embarking on a journey unlike any we had ever imagined. The current state of our war-torn home had rendered life unbearable, never knowing when more bombs would drop, struggling to keep basic necessities on hand, and seeing the country's infrastructure, especially the schools, either closed or ruined. Reluctantly, we made the heartbreaking decision to flee our home—a place that no longer felt like our own anymore.

In my heart, I yearned to depart—but only if we could return to the Yemen we knew before the war. My love for Yemen endured, even when it became too difficult to stay. There was real danger in traveling anywhere, and I'd heard stories of families stuck at the border.The Saudi borders were shut, and the news showed people stuck there because they didn't have the right papers. I felt relieved knowing we had the proper paperwork and following the rules could make things easier.

That day, we had lunch, unaware it might be our last meal for the next two days. Then we boarded a bus to the Saudi border, hoping it would take us to Al-Wadiah crossing. After eight hours , we reached only as far as Al-Abr in Hadramout, still two hours away from the Saudi border.

The driver stopped for a break and told us to rest. It was 3 am, and we were exhausted, so we went to sleep without eating anything. We resumed our journey at six in the morning. Two hours later, the bus abruptly came to a halt again. We were still 10 miles from the Saudi border checkpoint, but outside, we saw Yemeni security officers firing at people attempting to cross without passports or legal documentation.This is where our driver decided to drop us off. We were supposed to be driven to the Saudi crossing, but despite our protests, he refused to continue and demanded that we disembark.

Imagine packing your whole life into suitcases, not knowing how long you'd be away or if your belongings would be safe if left behind. Needless to say, we had a lot of luggage! Now we were tasked with carrying it all for 10 miles in the scorching desert heat – what a challenge! And I know what you're thinking – suitcases have wheels. But imagine dragging those wheels in desert sand; it just made everything harder, especially with additional carry-ons. A lot of the suitcase wheels got stuck, a fight most of us couldn't handle. The strain on our hands, shoulders and wounded feet intensified with each step. My pink sparkly shoes were now stained with sand and blood. Despite our fatigue, we trudged on, occasionally pausing to catch our breath and desperately trying to flag down a ride along the way, Here's what I reported to my diary:

We trudged on, intermittently stopping to catch our breath, each pause revealing more pain in our exhausted limbs. On the road, everyone was exhausted. We couldn't endure it any longer.

Trying to arrange transportation for thirteen people with heavy luggage felt like relocating a small village. However, after a 5-mile walk in the desert, we finally managed to secure a ride for everyone and continued until we reached the Saudi crossing.

But even there, the sun was scorching, and the sand burned beneath us. There was nothing around but barren desert. My biggest wish was to have a sip of water and find cool shade. The longer we sat there, the intense heat made the need for water and shade even more pressing. Until an old man with an angelic face and a Bedouin accent approached us and opened his van. "You are all welcome to come inside and have some rest," he told us. He left the door open, and I bounced inside, my four young relatives—Mariam, Marwa, Aziza, and Khaled—following me.

As I relaxed a bit, I started thinking that fast deaths, like in bombings, might be better than slowly dying of thirst under the blazing desert sun. I'm not exaggerating; many people, especially pregnant women and babies, died in situations just like ours.

We bought large bottles of water from a store located about 10 miles away at the Yemeni border. Within minutes, the intense heat made the water almost boiling, but we drank it anyway, despite the stomach pain I felt with every sip.When the water was almost gone, we all shared what was left—not to completely quench our thirst, but to stay alive. It was a big change from my old life: in addition to almost dying of thirst, it was the first time I shared or drank from the same bottle as someone else.

There, in front of the crossing, like thousands of other Yemenis, we were tired of waiting. And like countless others, we continued to endure. I finally went up to a border guard, showing him all my papers, including my American passport, hoping it might help. "What about those of us with everything in order?" I asked him.
"A transit visa, and confirmed flights from Saudi Arabia? We're not staying there, we just want to get to the airport."

The guard responded with a mocking laugh. "Don't even dream of the crossing opening today," he told me. "We will not open." I still remember his face clearly, the smirk that made me turn my back and break into tears. I wish he knew the life I used to have, the lives that all of us here used to have. It might have made it a little harder to humiliate everyone. Or to watch so many slowly die every day.

At night, I looked up at the stars, clear and captivating and our only source of light. After 24 hours with no entry to the crossing, we started to wonder about where we would sleep. We were homeless for the first time in any of our lives. My grandmother found refuge inside that man's van, which was great. My body ached, and my hands trembled, marked red from the bags we'd carried on the long road. As the sun disappeared, I dipped my hands in the cooling sand. Meanwhile, my sister Marwa cried out, pleading for a mattress instead of sleeping on the hard ground. Years later, the experience shaped my perspective on homeless people, making me more sensitive to their struggles. Life has a way of putting you in unexpected situations.

In the morning, we stayed for a couple of hours but then decided just to go back to Sana'a. We couldn't handle conditions at the crossing anymore."

Returning to Sana'a

A month later,following our attempt to cross the border, my uncle proposed another try at reaching the border. We decided not to join them, and they proceeded without us—my parents, my twin sisters, my brother and I stayed behind. Surprisingly, they succeeded this time. As they departed, we decided to leave the cramped apartment and return to our own house. Three months in that palace was enough.

As we opted to stay in Sana'a at that time, we bid farewell to family and friends, each of us going our separate ways. I couldn't help but wonder if we'd ever have the chance to see them again.

"Dear diary,
Entering the seventh month of this war, the streets echo destruction at every turn. Those who left yearn to return, yet they fail to grasp that it's not the same place anymore.

Sometimes, I wish I could go back to the undamaged version of this place. And I wonder what cuts deeper: the ache of being away from home or the unsettling feeling of being a stranger within its borders. It's ironic how I once dismissed geography, a subject I never truly comprehended. Now, it haunts me. Today, I find myself grappling with its complexities, struggling with the borders that have separated me from friends and family.

In school, I thought I could just skip it, but it turns out you can never escape geography. Even when I try to spend time with the few friends remaining here, a fuel shortage or just the ongoing airstrikes usually get in the way. A friend wrote about this, when she couldn't attend a close friend's wedding:

"I never thought that the difficulties in our country would crush such simple dreams, ones that don't hurt or cost much. Yet, these dreams slip through our fingers."

People can't even have simple dreams, let alone bigger ones. The true essence of what dreams should be has faded. Now some just wish for an hour of electricity once a week. Or maybe every two weeks!"

Drowning

Months passed, and I found myself overwhelmed. It felt like I was losing who I used to be. My mind hit a standstill. I couldn't create art anymore, finding it painful to engage in the activities I once enjoyed. I was feeling trapped in a monotonous, very limited life I had no control over. Each day felt like a struggle. While I hoped my dreams might offer something new, they also disappointed me. Nightmares became a frequent occurrence, making me dread sleep. The only solace I found was in books and pouring my thoughts into my diaries.

"Dear Diary,
I'm feeling like I'm losing my mind. Something strange is happening to my brain—I've realized that I no longer can tell the difference between reality and dreams. Am I going crazy?

Last night, we all slept in the hallway between rooms when the airstrikes became intense. It's supposedly safer to sleep in a place without windows. I dreamt that the wall of my room collapsed. When I woke up, I was convinced it had happened. To my surprise, when I entered my room, I found the walls were still intact, and I was shocked to realize it was just a dream! This is happening more frequently, and it's making me question my sanity."

Sanaá → Cairo
Sanaá → C

Cairo

One day, we woke up to some surprising news during breakfast—my dad shared that Sana'a International Airport was reopening soon. He mentioned there was only one airline operating, offering two destinations: Egypt and Jordan. Excitedly, he informed us he had already booked our flights, set for a month later. But there was a hitch - the tickets were not guaranteed. Each plane needed approval from authorities before taking off. Our journey included a stop in Saudi Arabia, where they inspected names, luggage, and everything else. Any suspicion, and we might be sent back.

My dad emphasized keeping this information to ourselves. He didn't want a repeat of our first attempt at leaving, explaining our situation to everyone if this didn't work out. Despite the high cost of $1000 USD per ticket to Egypt (typically around $250 USD), totaling $6000 USD for a three-hour flight, we hoped this would be the key to leaving the war behind. Here's what I wrote in my diary:

"The long-awaited day arrived on November 22, 2015, marking nine months into the war. We were finally deciding to leave. Looking back, I'm thankful that five months ago, our first attempt didn't work, bringing me back to where I started.

These months have reshaped my understanding of home, perhaps correcting it. I recall the face of the border guard, and I wish I could tell him I'll cross the border this time without his help.

I went to my university to retrieve my transcript, and upon examining it, I was astonished to find that it lacked the Higher Education Ministry stamp. Despite informing the university of my need for verification as I was fleeing the country, they handed me the document with an explanation: our university's accreditation had been compromised due to the war. This revelation was a new shock for me, and I struggled to comprehend it, though I hoped it was just a temporary setback.

After investing so much time, effort, and $2500 USD per semester, I was handed a paper that indicated none of it would be recognized, all due to circumstances beyond my control.

In my last moments in the space I called "my room,"
enclosed by walls that held everything but my dreams, I
took a last look around. I wanted to leave everything as it
was — my acrylic paint box and pens on the desk, an
incomplete painting. It's not that I hope to return quickly
to finish that painting, but much the opposite, to return
very slowly.

Slow enough for me to forget who I was during this time,
slow enough to feel like I've stepped back in time, witnessing
a previous version of myself without the need of
a time-traveling machine.

We headed to the airport at eight in the morning because of the heightened security measures. After completing the procedures, we waited for the plane that would take us to our destinations—only two flights were available, one to Jordan and the other to Egypt. Instead of the usual speaker sounds at the airport, a man's voice echoed through the airport, loudly announcing the boarding of the flight to Amman, Jordan. However, a few minutes later, the same voice apologized, clarifying that he meant the Cairo flight. What caught my attention was someone who seemed indifferent to the confusion, just going with either flight. When asked about his destination, he replied, "Anywhere." It was the saddest yet most sarcastically real—time joke I had ever heard.

After waiting for eight hours, the plane finally took off at 5 pm and, after a short flight, stopped at the Saudi Bisha airport for two hours. I was waiting to find that border guard there, knowing I wouldn't see him but wanting to anyway. We finally arrived in Cairo after midnight. It was a full day of travel for a trip that would usually take about three hours. But at least we made it out this time."

Now what?

When I was in the middle of the war, I believed that leaving it would solve all my problems. But once we got to Egypt, I felt strangely disconnected from reality. I kept asking myself, "Now what?"

Things didn't automatically go back to normal, as I had envisioned. I thought once I left, everything would fall back into place. But that wasn't the case. During our first months in Egypt, my family and I were in a sort of touristy mode. My dad initially said we'd be there for a maximum of three months and then return to Yemen when things settled. Despite trying to relax and enjoy ourselves, everything felt meaningless, and sometimes, I even felt guilty being anywhere or doing anything. Small, unexpected things triggered big, overwhelming emotions.

Coping with life after the war would be harder than I'd thought. My family and I were among the fortunate ones. We didn't endure visible physical injuries or significant losses. No one in my extended family suffered serious harm or extended disabilities. But the impact on our lives has been undeniable.

I feel compelled to discuss this because, even without obvious physical injuries, it's never easy to simply resume life after experiencing a war. Instead, we've had the challenge of starting new lives with a sense of normality — while showing no trace of what we've been through. Every day, we pretend that the war is behind us — even though it still lives in our hearts and our minds.

For me, our good fortune only underscores what others have suffered, those who've endured even more horrendous conditions.I know their pain must run even deeper, regardless of the wounds the rest of us might not see.I remember experiencing daily panic attacks triggered by seemingly random things. Cairo -- a crowded, densely populated place with a lot of noises -- made it even more difficult. The first apartment we
rented was relatively old, and for some reason, the sound of doors closing and windows squeezing shut mimicked the sounds in our house before the bombings. I was surprised that I was triggered by these sounds. I assumed my brain knew that I wasn't in Yemen now and there wasn't a war happening here in Cairo. But my brain wasn't convinced. Everyday sounds -- airplanes, buses, the metro, and even fireworks -- triggered panic attacks.

"Dear Diary,
I'm sitting alone here on my balcony, facing the Nile River.
I wonder why I'm here, at this specific time and place.
A year ago, if someone said I'd be in Cairo, I'd think of family trips that end with returning home. It's not that I want to go back; living in Yemen started to feel like being in a huge prison lately. I don't hate Yemen, but I can't live there. And I feel like I have left gradually.

I left Yemen long before physically leaving. I don't miss it yet because I got used to living without feeling at home. I don't know where I'll settle, but dealing with challenges elsewhere feels easier than waiting for that war to allow me to live.

I'm just 20 years old, I crave the life I've imagined. I want to experience different days, I still have so much to do, and so much to say, I want to give life meaning. Those who make war have no dreams and tend to steal ours out of envy.

Every morning, I remind myself not to long for that place. I find comfort in believing the sky here is as blue. I just remind myself to not be fooled by homeland-scented poetry; oxygen is the same everywhere.

For me, longing for home in this situation feels like missing someone who has already passed away. Memories rush back, tempting you to go back and relive precious moments. But when you return, you face irreversible changes, realizing that what you long for now is gone forever, buried in the ground. This deepens the pain even more, which is why I don't want to go back."

FUN CITY

Fun City

After three months in Cairo, having left the war behind, we're always keeping an eye on what's happening in Yemen. We consistently check on the people we know who are still there, keeping ourselves in limbo between the life we currently have and the life we've put on hold. It's a strange feeling, this in-between state. On one hand, we've physically moved away from the immediate danger of the war, creating a semblance of a new life. But our hearts remain tethered to the place and the people we left behind. The constant updates and news from there keep us connected, creating a bridge between two worlds. This state of being stuck in between is a challenging space to navigate.

While we strive to build a new life and move forward, the ties to our past experiences, the people we care about, and the place we once called home continue to hold a significant place in our hearts and minds. It's a delicate balance of embracing the present while carrying the weight of an unresolved past, making each step forward a sometimes bittersweet journey.

"Dear Diary,

Today, while scrolling through my social media, I stumbled upon a place I knew all too well. In Sana'a, where entertainment spots were few and could be counted on fingers, Fun City Amusement Park stood out as one of the most cherished places.Seeing images of its wreckage today triggered a flood of memories.

During our last days in Sana'a during the war, we made it a weekly ritual to visit Fun City Park. It was one of the few places that made us feel the pulse of life. We never saw big crowds, but when we were there, we were determined to have fun, even when bombings were a regular threat.

Fun City was only open four days a week and just five hours a day. But every worker took charge of two rides, and we ignored everything, simply living in the moment. Seeing families celebrating birthdays, candles casting a sparkle in their eyes, with the laughter of friends echoing around, I couldn't help but come back with memories every time I visited.

I remember my first visit, trying my hand at bowling for the first time. I didn't give the ball enough force, and it stopped at the beginning of the lane. My friend joked the ball wouldn't complete the journey on its own.

Before the war, we often spent summer break there, creating some of our best memories. Now, I'm left wondering if these memories are lost forever. The war seems to be erasing the memories we've gathered over the years in a matter of minutes. Isn't it a heartbreaking thought? I can't help but wonder if, the next time I see Sana'a, I'll even recognize it."

I'll play with you

I suddenly remembered "Shams"

I was recently reminiscing about Shams, an Iraqi friend from my fifth-grade days. I vividly recall disliking playing with her; she approached games with an unexpected intensity that belied her delicate appearance. Her favorite game involved clapping our hands together while singing peculiar Arabic lyrics that vaguely translated to something like, "Play with me, I'll play with you until our fingers get broken." And, oddly enough, she took that part quite literally. Our play sessions always ended with my hands red and sore.

I realized it was the first time in my life that I had a friend named Shams. Her name meant "sun" in Arabic, and she'd arrived in the middle of the semester—an unusual time to introduce a new student to the class. All eyes were on her, but contrary to her name, she wasn't radiating like the sun. She kept her head low, resembling a sunset more than anything else. A teacher accompanied her, introducing her as "Shams from Iraq, seeking refuge from the war." As soon as the word "war" was uttered, Shams burst into tears, her face tinged red. In that moment, the significance of her name became evident. She was radiating intense anger and sorrow.

If she were with me today, I'd apologize to Shams. I didn't know her little heart was burning from the inside. I wish we could play again, until our hands, hearts and minds go numb. I hope we can someday, losing ourselves in the moment.

ERROR
404
home youre looking
For is not Found
Try again ?

What is home

Ahmed Matar, the poet, once said:

"We die for our homeland to live!
But for whom?
Once we're gone, it's just dust and gloom.
We are the homeland."

Ahmed Matar's words left me puzzled until recently. When I say I miss home now, I'm also not talking about a piece of land. But my idea of home is less about dust and gloom and more about a stable life, free from time constraints, filled with the warmth of friends' embraces, the laughter of family, and a soul at peace. Like Matar, I also have a sense of absence, knowing that all of that can be lost in a moment.

For me, home has always been a bit tricky. I was born in the United States but left when I was 4. Most of my growing up happened in different parts of the Middle East, because my family kept moving. As a kid, I often wondered what home meant because I never felt like I fit in anywhere.

My parents would say we're originally from Yemen, where they're from, but it felt like an imaginary connection since I hadn't been there. Over time, though, I started feeling attached to this place I didn't yet know.I still remember proudly telling a kid in kindergarten that I'm from Yemen, just like my parents taught me. But the next day, he said his mom,a geography teacher, told him there's no country with that name. I cried to my mom, questioning if Yemen was a real place. A year later, we started visiting Yemen every summer, creating the best childhood memories with my cousins. As I grew up, my connection to Yemen became stronger.

In 2004, my family decided to move to Yemen, and we bought our first house. I lived there for the most stable 11 years of my life until the war in 2015. Everything changed after the war, and I found myself asking the same question I had at 5: What is home? I felt like a stranger in my own land, and it wasn't the same place I lovedanymore. It became a place I barely recognized. That's when I realized home isn't just a place; it's a feeling, and I haven't felt home since then.

2017
2016
2015

Weeks turned into months and months into years

As we stayed in Egypt, weeks turned into months, and months turned into years. In the initial two years, I grappled with the aftermath of war trauma and post-war depression. Deep down, I yearned to resume a normal life and return to school, but the reality I faced had different plans, making it challenging to get back on track.

People often questioned why we didn't just go back to the US since my dad and siblings were American citizens. But my mom didn't have US citizenship, and there was a ban on Yemenis coming at that time. So, we decided to remain in the same place. In the third year of my stay in Egypt, I learned about the Yemeni Cultural Center, conveniently located within walking distance from my home. An announcement caught my attention: free drawing classes for Yemenis led by the renowned Yemeni artist Radfan Almohammadi. Intrigued, I decided to attend, and it turned out to be a transformative experience.I formed connections with amazing people, even spotting a Yemeni actress whom I used to see on TV.

After attending for a few months, people got to know me, and they discovered my background in graphic design. They suggested that I lead the next course, teaching Yemeni refugees some basic graphic design skills. Despite not being a pro, I shared what I knew. Since the place lacked computers, the only requirement was to bring your own laptop. I didn't expect many participants, but to my surprise, people showed up, and watching their progress was incredibly rewarding. Teaching them a skill they could continue to use and learn from, possibly leading to income, was fulfilling.

Suddenly, I felt like myself again, surrounded by creative and inspiring individuals, reconnecting with the things I've always loved. This experience pushed me to break free from the plans I had in my head. I let go of returning to traditional academics and embraced this new path with a profoundly positive impact.

The same year, I also got engaged and began planning for my wedding the following year. I had always believed I wouldn't get married until I graduated college, but I was starting to let go of my rigid plans. I was starting to go with the flow, to give space for magic to happen. Every time I'd clung to my plans, I found myself hurt when life unfolded differently.

• Live

I wish I were there
This is not fair

My Wedding Day

In the aftermath of the war, many events brought unexpected triggers. I remember arguing with my mom about skipping wedding party because the people I truly wanted there couldn't attend. Convincing a typical Arab mom to forgo celebrating the wedding of her first daughter proved to be no easy task. In the end, I decided to go through with the wedding primarily for her, even though my reservations lingered.

Traditional Arab weddings are known for their grandiosity, often hosting around 1000 guests. In contrast, my wedding was relatively small, with about 170 attendees, mostly invited by my outgoing and socially connected mom, who, within just three years, had built numerous relationships in Cairo. On the flip side, my guest list consisted of around 10 people. As I entered the wedding venue, surrounded by a sea of unfamiliar faces, I couldn't shake the feeling of how much more enjoyable it would be with the friends I had always imagined sharing such happy moments with. Sadly, they weren't present physically; instead, they witnessed my wedding live online from different locations. They sent a cake adorned with all their photos, a gesture that made the day even more emotional.

DEPARTMENT OF HOMELAND SECURITY • U.S. CUSTOMS AND BORDER PROTECTION
ADMITTED
DEC 2 5 2018
10
7191
Class
Until

Coming back to US

Although I was born in the US, I never felt a deep connection to the place. I left when I was only four years old, and my memories of that time are scarce. They consist of a few videos my dad used to take of me and my siblings, but they're sort of blended with the images of the US that I've seen in movies. Over time, these elements merged in my mind, creating a collection of thoughts that I believed were my memories.

Although I've moved around quite a bit, mostly within Arab countries, this new experience is different. It's interesting to note how different everything is—people speak differently, think differently, and even the measurement system is unfamiliar. It's not a big deal, but I recall a funny incident in the US when my college misunderstood my birthdate format. They thought I might not be the same person in their records because I was accustomed to writing it as day, month, year, while here it's month, day, year. Little cultural shocks like that have been part of the journey.

I remember my initial fascination with individuality here, a contrast to the group-based society I come from. It felt liberating, thinking I could do whatever I wanted without nosy neighbors reporting every move.

Back home, people are deeply involved in each other's business, and while it's a form of care, it can be overwhelming sometimes. Yet, over the years, I've learned to appreciate the balance. There was a turning point when I found myself in a potentially dangerous situation. Despite it being broad daylight, I was confronted by a homeless woman wielding a large glass bottle. Despite her clear aggression and vocal threats of harm, nobody intervened. This alarming experience prompted deep reflection on the sense of community I had always associated with home. It brought to mind an incident when I had a minor car accident back in Yemen, and strangers stopped to help, offering assistance and even money. Despite telling them I had everything under control, their willingness to help was in stark contrast to the incident here. It made me feel a bit out of place. I'm not implying that people here are bad; it's just that societal norms are different, which might not be a big deal if you've never lived in a more community-based culture.

I'm grateful for the second chance, the new beginning I've had in the US. My journey began at a community college, where my pursuit of an associate's degree stretched across four years. A hiatus, prompted by the birth of my son and the tumult of the 2019 COVID situation, interrupted my coursework. Online classes added yet another layer of complexity too. When I finally graduated from community college, it felt like it took an eternity. But it hit me like a tidal wave.

Walking past the stands at my graduation, accompanied by the haunting melody of a violin, my eyes scanned the crowd of proud parents, siblings, and friends. In the sea of faces, I glimpsed a man who bore a striking resemblance to my father. He even shouted from the stands, "This is my daughter." He wasn't my father, but in that moment, I wanted to claim him as my own. I had to fight back tears, but my soul felt unbroken. My soul, resilient against the ravages of war, post-war depression, the challenges of motherhood, and a global pandemic, found strength in persisting for a singular reason.

And I saw that reason at the top of the stands, a man with a small child on his shoulders, my husband, radiating a loving presence. I sensed his smile far away when I nodded his way. Memories flooded back — moments when this man took my hand and supported me unconditionally. He even accompanied me to my first classes, easing my transition into this new educational realm.

In dark times, he emerged as my sole source of light and unwavering support. For a fleeting moment, his eyes, brimming with pride, were enough to make me smile. At that moment, my husband and my son, along with my only brother living here, were my crowd, and they were enough.

I'm glad you SURVIVED
I'm glad you are Safe now

Have I ever survived war?

I find myself uttering the words, "I'm a war survivor," when asked to share a fun fact about myself. It's become a social experiment of sorts, gauging people's reactions. Very few display genuine surprise, and that used to anger me. Is it so ingrained in the general public that people who look like me should be so causally, so obviously associated with war?

I use the phrase "war survivor" frequently, but I question if I ever truly survived, and I think about that almost every day. I hear people trying to be comforting, saying stuff like, "I'm glad you're safe now." But that always leads me to think: Am I safe? Because I feel like I'm never safe from the impact war has had on my life.

Survival isn't a straightforward path; it's not just about whether you survive or not. Surviving is a complex gray area that takes on various forms and shapes. Some may seem to have physically survived because the damage isn't visible to you.

Others mightappear to be leading normal lives after the war as if they've successfully moved on. But the reality is that the effects of war continue to impact them every single day, even years after they've physically left the battlefield.

War isn't an experience you survive; I've even come to view it the opposite way. I feel that the only people who survive war are the ones who perished in it. No one who has been in a war can escape the clutches of war; it lives within you every day. I can't recall a single day in almost the past decade without thoughts of what transpired. Almost everything around me and every decision in my life has somehow been impacted by war. That annoyed me for a long time, because even when I tried to run from it, war still held its grip, controlling so much of my life.

I get reminders all the time. I'm reminded when my boss, younger than me, boasts a master's degree on his wall – a stark reminder of the years stolen by war, before I could resume my life again. Every holiday is a reminder that my family is scattered globally, fighting different time zones for a mere phone call. Even when I had my son, the war was still with me. My mom wasn't around for it, like I'd always pictured. I was reminded when my son saw my family for the first time, already a year-and-a-half old. They missed all his infant stages, and he didn't know who they were.I'm reminded of war when I see my son missing the joy I had playing with my extensive network of cousins. I get reminded when other wars start anywhere.

I'm reminded every day, all the time – walking, driving, eating. Perhaps, I never truly survived war; maybe no one survives it, but it continues somewhere, an unrelenting force shaping lives and destinies. War is happening now as I write this, and war is happening now as you are reading this, and it sadly never stops. I remember how I used to get so angry that the world just continues, that the globe keeps spinning, that people just go on with their daily lives.

Talking about war makes everyone uncomfortable, but for every untold story, a part of the war experience remains buried, unheard, and the urgency to exhume these narratives becomes paramount. The weight of unspoken truths festers, perpetuating the cycle of incomprehension and detachment. Our collective voices, the strength of our shared narratives, can become a beacon against the darkness.

Afterall, the more we talk about the lives affected by war, the less it sounds like political discourse; it is a human imperative. Our stories, those etched in pain, resilience, and survival, serve as a testament to those that remain untold, the brave individuals navigating the harshest terrains of human conflict. Through these narratives, we confront the paradoxes of war—the strength it extracts and the fragility it reveals. And the ordinary people described in these stories, they're each a microcosm of the human experience, beckoning us to engage in conversations that transcend borders, ideologies and politics. They urge us to tear down our most common barriers, whatever keeps us from embracing the humanity that binds us all. In this crescendo, I hope you can hear a call to action, a plea to shatter the silence that allows wars to persist. Every story, every tear-stained confession, becomes a testament to the resilience of the human spirit and a plea for collective acknowledgment.

As you close this book, let the emotions stirred within you catalyze change. Let them propel you into a world where conversations about war are not relegated to the sidelines but take center stage. The human experience during war, with all its complexities, deserves to be heard, understood and shared. For it is in the telling of these stories that we forge connections, build bridges, and, ultimately, pave the way for a future where the echoes of war are replaced by the harmonious cadence of c ollective empathy and understanding.

Download the Zapper App on your phone and scan this code with it to browse the real footage AR gallery.